The Right Home

Becca Heddle

OXFORD
UNIVERSITY PRESS

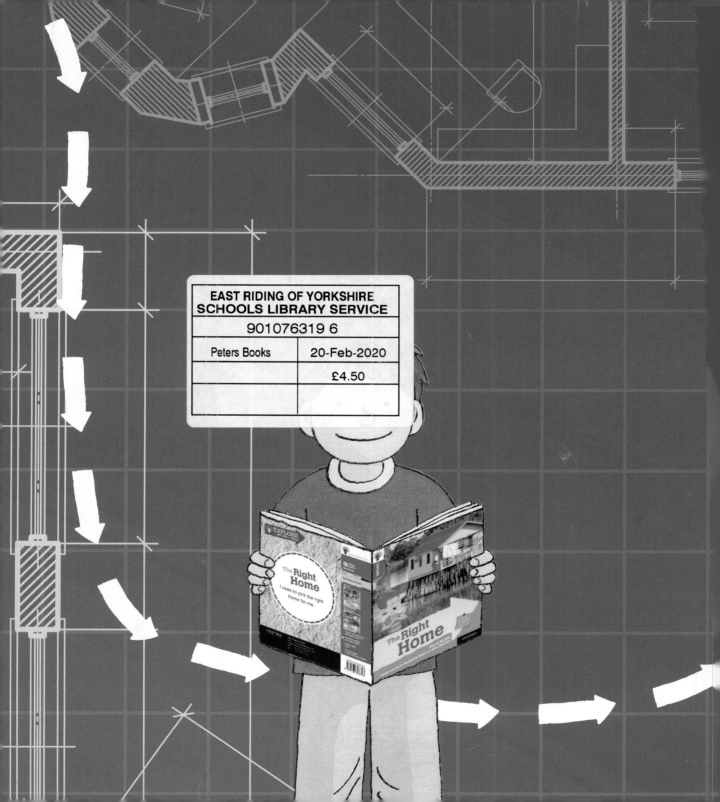

Contents

This home is fun. It has plants on the roof.

6

This home is too high up for me.

Pick a home that is right for you:

roof of plants

home in a tree

home in the rock

home on stilts

tent

canal boat

Look Back, Explorers

How do you get to the home in the tree?

What must the boy's home be near?

Why do you think a home on stilts is good if you live by a river?

Did you find out where this home is?

Explorer Challenge: in a tree (page 9)

What's Next, Explorers?

Now read about what happens when Biff, Chip and Kipper go to a different home for a night …

Explorer Challenge
for *Home for a Night*

Where does this ladder go?